GRAYBEARD WHISPERS

t. kilgore splake
25214 ash street
calumet, mi 49913

TRANSCENDENT ZERO PRESS
HOUSTON, TEXAS

PUBLISHED BY TRANSCENDENT ZERO PRESS
www.transcendentzeropress.org

ISBN-13: 978-1-946460-19-6

Printed in the United States of America

Transcendent Zero Press
16429 El Camino Real Apt. #7
Houston, TX 77062

Cover photos: t. kilgore splake

FIRST EDITION

GRAYBEARD WHISPERS

t. kilgore splake
25214 ash street
calumet, mi 49913

INTRODUCTION

The creative concept of whispering is not new. A whisper implies many things. In a sense, it is quietude in the midst of something holy. In another sense, it is subtlety because it acts on the underlying senses. Because a whisper is a secretive thing, it's nature is something akin to grief. These poems by t. kilgore splake remind us why we grieve: ultimately, we grieve for our losses as they become distant from us. We lose everything over time. Youth, for instance, passes into age and we become frail and forgetful.

t. kilgore splake uses his impressionistic approach to poetry to compose a diary of watching the aging as it happens. His poems take place in the present where action is most important. However, he invokes historical context such as the tragedy of 9/11 to remind us that life is something grand and mysterious. In poems such as "beginning life again" we are reminded of Nature's own grief within Her paradise. Several of these poems invoke the wilderness, shadows, fishing, and the intriguing life beyond civilization. splake himself adopts the pen name as a localized tribute to the wildlife. The solitary life of an artist is one in defiance of reason and society as the opening poems indicate. The poem "becoming a poet" reiterates this point. Is there a reason we should explain to anyone, including ourselves, why we create when life itself seems devoid of such a purpose? God does not explain his beginning to us. He offers no reason but the great "I AM".

A whisper can pass through without anyone noting it. It is a quick visitor. It also harbors the ancient past. Nature whispers in the wind through the trees. A whisper is a dark but delicate thing. This explains our mortality—we are living fossils of life. We pass and leave ourselves with the world in the form of art, children, legacy, or another one of our human ways of being immortal. Although we grow old and pass into the dirt, there is something to be said of who we were and still are.

graybeard whispers is another one of life's many legacies.

Dustin Pickering, publisher

suits

lawyer realtor accountant
undertaker selling
coffin and cemetery lot
# # # #

non-poet

never misspelling words
checking account always balanced
without creative thoughts
# # # #

brautigan creek magic

inside forest shadows
quiet inner peace
rippling energy of life
# # # #

just taking a walk

leaving footprints
on wilderness path
forgotten pleasure
# # # #

chill

tender young lips
naked young flesh
mouth soft and salty
# # # #

coltrane jazz

start with music's middle
move from beginning to end
both directions at once
# # # #

topographic map

elevation brown lines
blue bodies of water
not explaining territory
# # # #

olde shoppe

summer tourist trap
t-shirts and postcards
pottery ashtrays
stuffed animals
local poet's book
# # # #

love's finish

after she said
"let's be friends"
sinking to knees
painful choking breaths
dry-heaving in toilet
# # # #

splake fishing service

calvary cemetery
hungover poets
three lonely daughters
olga x-pat's ghost
secret lover gwyneth
sobbing over grave
# # # #

coming of age

50's childhood
obeying the rules
becoming young gentlemen
ladylike behaviors
today's thirteen year olds
done it all
# # # #

forest music

trees whispering secrets
hum and chirp of insects
light afternoon breeze
carrying soft birdsong
wilderness symphony
without instrument sounds
# # # #

minnesota fats

cue ball kiss
reverse english spin
hustling eight-ball
down green felt rail
side pocket victory
fast eddie felton dream
# # # #

ah and so

student's complaint
can't do what i want
with minister dad
serious professor's reply
imagine having father
school's football coach
# # # #

escape

lost in cliffs horizon
lake superior tides
vast wilderness foliage
forgotten last time
focusing on beauty
away from computer screen
# # # #

darkness

denying lethal pill
for dying poet friend
ending aids suffering
afraid of death
quiet hospital vigil
both waiting relief
that never comes
# # # #

choice

deciding against chemo
possibly six more months
puking in hospital bucket
instead sitting on cliffs
watching superior tides
floating in clouds
slowly drifting away
# # # #

only one winner

cold winds against
mountain climber's shadow
corrida's matador
loud el toro oles
fans cheering fighters
boxing ring canvas
music of battle and death
# # # #

paula

late dark nights
quiet early mornings
feeling your presence
momentary passing shadow
brought by past angers
memories of warm passions
mad ghost lover
# # # #

journey into mystery

poet's quiet shadow
solitary forest silhouette
light breeze blowing
pine scents wafting
wildflower aromas fading
shotgun oiled
double xx load
# # # #

living in the light

climbing cliffs at night

leaving darkness below

moving slowly up path

muscle-mental memories

moon breaking through clouds

lighting summit shadows

poet coming home

living in the light

# # # #

poet

black beret

john lennon glasses

turtleneck and levis

dark bushy beard

always carrying notebook

baristas serving

early morning espresso

quietly whispering quirky

# # # #

carpe diem

vogue vanity fair glamour
mall shopping sprees
fashion clothes horse
desperately buying disguises
hiding inner self
instead being vulnerable
meeting touching loving
another human being
soul coming alive
# # # #

underground dues

artistic world not caring
about creative truth
beauty in the world
interested only in markets
making more money
writers and poets
eagerly selling out
small price to pay
for momentary celebrity
# # # #

beginning life again

fierce arctic blizzard
dark howling gale
continuous white swirls
snow drifting higher
covering familiar world
like lost horizons
hiding shangri-la
waking to discover
brave new world
# # # #

memorial day ghosts

guadalcanal and iwo
bataan death march
omaha beach
ardennes winter bulge
forgotten young men
gold stars now gray
front window banner
lost in old diaries
family bibles
dusty attic corners
# # # #

salad days

college degree
professor with career
attractive wife
discussing family
son daughter names
new car color television
like cody jarret
on top of the world
brief early time
you could do anything
# # # #

latte prisoner

mama cass monday
rosetta coffee shop
bitchy barista
ugly black mood
taking no shit
from hungover salesmen
national park rangers
jehovah's witnesses
graybeard poet
# # # #

facing future

poet's shadow floating
on dark early mists
surveying the horizon
lost in haunting depression
choosing 12-gauge solution
moving in stillness
to brightly lit place
home without name
where life ends
# # # #

holier than thou

heaven sounds boring
normal ordinary place
tennis and golf
replacing pool tables
serious eight-ball games
afternoon tea
chilled lemonade
instead of cheap wine
twist off caps
mad dog 20-20 rush
# # # #

journey through nature

dark poet's shadow
passing through thicket
dense forest puckerbrush
following deer run
rising through wilderness
moving above tree line
reaching summit
tall granite retreat
deep serious karma
leading solitary artist
to where life ends
# # # #

hannah's father

walking family dog
cleaning bird cage
changing fish tank water
buying oils and canvas
charcoal pens
vellum drawing tablets
purchasing art books
coffee table remainders
creative time-life series
giving daughter
precious time to create
learning about making art
# # # #

dying at home

artist friend

greatest generation brother

eighty-five year old

falling from ladder

cleaning snow

off studio roof

breaking his leg

suddenly lost

in nursing home hell

his close friend

afraid of death

not helping

old painter escape

# # # #

not a baby anymore

high ponytail
small perky tits
mirror reflecting
slender naked body
thick lip gloss
patchouli perfume
wearing sexy clothes
blink and its over
large ugly veins
couple of extra chins
wrinkled pale skin
thin graying hair
white scalp spots
forgetting her name
# # # #

becoming a poet

struggling for consciousness
after writing first poem
like leaving dark womb
rising from fresh grave
climbing out of deep pit
wondering about future
abandoning affluent life
monthly wrestling credit
after buying more things
worried finding words
filling blank page
explaining to others
why writing poems
important thing in life
# # # #

google daily medico

checking computer screen
after morning metamucil
worrying about clogged arteries
good and bad cholesterol
strokes and heart attacks
reading recent obituaries
words seeming blurry
time for cataract surgery
checking for car keys
alzheimer's memory lapse
sharp arthritic pains
no aspirin or tylenol
body pissing blood
from medicine allergy
mysterious graying fates
golden years passing

# # # #

no longer young

rocking chair miles
nights with crying baby
after children
wife lost her libido
letting looks go
constantly nagging
frustrated husband
tired of jacking off
drinking too much
fat beer belly
prisoner in suburbs
boring same old shit
working for years
dying before retirement
needing touch or taste
mad wild adventure
another chance at life

# # # #

beyond class reunion

graybeard poet
like chance wayne
paul newman character
returning home
renewing memories
of high school days
reminiscing with
senior prom date
football team mates
being himself
not prisoner of
other peoples thinking
time running out
final chance
to write honest poem
rare original creation
baccalaureate
before passing on
# # # #

stumbling over memories

sunny sandbox days
old apple tree swing
summer lasting forever
kindergarten nap rugs
old classroom desks
wooden lids and inkwells
high school athletics
playing different ball games
chasing pretty girls
cheerleader's sweetheart
never making honor roll
marriages families divorces
things people do
suddenly graying
with rat bastard time
now confused over
yesterday and last week
unworried about tomorrow
life same every day
# # # #

taking no prisoners

mental health weekend
professor escaping classroom
upper peninsula odyssey
driving ford bronco
over old logging trails
dusty clouds
covering rearview mirror
cold six pack
traveling companion
pissing in puckerbrush
car door open
engine running
taking deep breath
pure chilly air
quiet solitary hours
happy and free
soon returning
miles below the bridge
back to academia
feeling refreshed

# # # #

odyssey

leaving black birds
circling the cliffs
riding warm thermals
floating with clouds
moving across the sky
forest wilderness
farmer's fields
cities and houses
rivers lakes streams
distant shadows below
while roots and worms
eating flesh and bones
turning body remains
into fresh earth
spirit of poet
continuing final journey
finding new existence
beyond the stars
coming home to himself
# # # #

wilderness companions

brautigan tree paperbacks
no shredder ending
not dusty used
bookstore shelf copies
forgotten in attics
storage room shadows
dissolving into nature
rain sun wind
long northern winters
seasons of long white
so richard's wisdom
gentle loving humor
will be in the earth
company for splake ghost
also for future
brautigan creek visitors
as uncle walt said
creative ideas
magnificent poems
resting under boot soles
# # # #

betrayal

mister nice guy
not seeking vengeance
hiring witch or warlock
using black arts
imposing spell or curse
personal betrayal
suffering from dementia
satisfactory revenge
reading a book
watching new movie
sadly memories
erased in the mornings
becoming virgin again
learning about sex
without the cojones
to pass over with glory
as leapers did
during twin-tower flames
or sit on stump
beside brautigan creek
with .357 magnum
looking in god's eyes
whispering welcome to heaven
# # # #

yesterday

nighttime shadows
poet's mind drifting
quiet pre-rem moment
remembering greenwich village
small basement bistro
bleeker street location
spaghetti dinner
with dark-hair young girl
warm candle glow
wax dripping down
empty chianti bottle
soft piano sounds
distant café corner
musician playing for drinks
toasting shadowy ghosts
early village bohemians
whitman lowell eugene oneill
salvador dali pollock warhol
whisper of beats
kerouac and ginsberg
sharing past dreams
of tortured imaginations
sadness of many
forgotten broken souls

\# \# \# \#

journey

finding secret path
off cliffs trail
not listed on maps
like harry potter
escaping to hogwart's
slipping through depot platform
nine and three quarters
climbing to granite summit
inspecting old copper mine
huge poor-rock piles
finding brautigan garden
place of special magic
reading verses
on wilderness poet tree
locating forest library
with collected titles
kerouac papa hem fitzgerald
large old brautigan pine
"trout fishing in america"
richard's other paperbacks
old rocking chair
convenient tin cup
for slaking visitor's thirsts
choosing small stone
bright shiny pebble

stream's sandy bed

mysterious talisman

bringing good luck

quiet woodland retreat

with peace and harmony

exciting mysteries

of poet frosts'

less traveled way

brief opportunity

celebrating the soul

# # # #

9 781946 460196